# A Treasury of MODEL RAILROAD PHOTOS

## FOUR CREATIVE APPROACHES TO MODEL RAILROAD PHOTOGRAPHY

### BY DAVE FRARY, MALCOLM FURLOW, JOHN OLSON, AND PAUL SCOLES

EDITOR: Mark Hembree
ASSISTANT EDITORS: Marcia Stern
Michael Emmerich
ART DIRECTOR: Lawrence O. Luser
ARTISTS: Phil Kirchmeier
Mark Watson

KALMBACH BOOKS

# INTRODUCTION

Scale models have a special magic that fires the imagination. It's hard to explain this magic, but there is ample evidence that it exists. One of the most popular exhibits at the 1939 New York World's Fair was the General Motors Futurama Pavilion, which featured a 3,000-square-foot scale model of New York City. At the 1964 New York World's Fair, General Motors again presented a Futurama — a model of a city of the future. Again, it was one of the most popular exhibits. The favorable response speaks well of a scale model's ability to communicate.

If you agree that a picture is worth a thousand words, then you can understand how photographing a model railroad amplifies its "message." We (the authors) took up photography after our modelbuilding skills were established, and we regard photography and model railroading as parts of the same hobby. We welcome the opportunity to share our interest visually with those who can't personally visit our railroads.

What makes a good model railroad photo? Certainly, having nice models and scenery helps, but what contributes most is our perception of a scene. Good photos are seen in the mind's eye first. We construct our scenes and dioramas with the camera in mind.

When a modeler takes camera in hand, he begins to make choices. Which film? What lighting? Where should the camera be placed? What aperture and shutter speed will capture all of the graduated tones and minute detail of a fine miniature locomotive or landscape?

Indeed, model railroad photography presents special problems. All of us create our photos under similar circumstances. We take ultra-close photos in difficult environments. The cramped quarters of a typical model railroad room (often a basement or attic) present technical limitations and hazards that are not found elsewhere. Our work area is usually small and hot, and always hard to light. When you consider the copious amounts of film and foul language used, the results are surprisingly pleasant.

In explaining our work we have assumed that the reader possesses a basic knowledge of photography. If you are new to the art of using a 35 mm camera, or don't know what an *f*-stop is, enjoy the pictures but consult other books for an introduction to photography. *How to Photograph Scale Models*, by Lane Stewart and Sheperd Paine (Kalmbach), is a great place to start learning the basics of model photography. Also, Kodak publishes an excellent workshop series of books on basic photography.

While this is not a technical guide to photography, we hope you'll glean a better understanding of photography techniques by looking over our shoulders at our favorite railroads. Sometimes a complex concept can be understood better by placing it in a familiar context.

We'll show you some fancy and complex methods, as well as how to create enjoyable photos with inexpensive equipment and props. You don't need years of schooling or a lot of money to get the camera to see things your way. In fact, you may be surprised to find how often the main ingredient in a great photo is luck!

**Perhaps the best-known model railroad ever, the HO scale Gorre & Daphetid was the life work of John Allen. Ironically, fire destroyed John's railroad shortly after his death in 1973 — but his many photos of the G&D survived to inspire model railroaders and photographers. This book is dedicated to the memory of John Allen — model railroader and photographer.**

4 DAVE FRARY

# A land of make-believe

## DAVE FRARY

I've been fascinated by trains ever since I was old enough to climb onto the dresser and look out my bedroom window at the Boston & Maine tracks behind my house. When I was old enough to venture outside, my mother had to tie me to the fence to keep me from playing on the main line. From that vantage point I could still watch the trains pass. World War Two had just ended, and the railroad traffic was varied and busy.

Like many boys in the early 1950s, my introduction to model railroading was a Lionel train. Later, I graduated to HO scale. I liked it because it tracked well and kept running. I also dabbled in HOn3 and HOn2. Neither of these narrow gauges would track or operate reliably (I was a sloppy builder), but they offered more opportunities for scratchbuilding and fantasizing.

In the late '60s, spurred on by my friend (and now Kalmbach editor) Bob Hayden, I investigated HOn2½. A new world opened to me. I could model my favorite narrow gauge prototypes, the Maine two-foot railroads, using N gauge track, turnouts, wheels, and mechanisms. Best of all, it required little more than routine maintenance.

Photography motivated me to improve my building techniques — nothing shows defects in a model like a close-up photo! My models and the railroads they were placed on became more detailed for the sake of the camera.

In fact, my whole railroad has turned into one giant photo prop. Areas are constantly changed to suit new or different photo angles. On some models I build only the sides that will be photographed, spending a great deal of time painting to accent shadows and detail. I've even cut a structure in half to get just the right shot to illustrate an article!

My trains don't look like the real thing, but like well-crafted models —which is what they are.

---

**Sometimes I get lucky! Every model railroad photographer strives to fill the frame with trains that lead the viewer's eye through the scene. In this photo on Bill Aldrich's New Haven layout, the curving tracks and high camera angle provide the composition — the trains do the rest. The natural colors of Bill's models enhance the realism.**

## CAMERA/LENS COMBINATIONS

There is no single camera/lens combination that works best for close-up model photography. I have adapted standard equipment to my particular needs. I based my choice of equipment on what I could afford (which was little or nothing) and what I thought I needed (lots of the best of everything), studying ads and keeping notebooks on camera models and prices. Through trials and many errors I got my collection of odds and ends to produce decent model photos.

In the early '50s, my favorite (rich) uncle loaned me a 35 mm Zeiss Contaflex camera, a tripod (which I still use), a General Electric exposure meter, several photo books, and a set of movie lights. The Zeiss was the first single-lens reflex camera I had ever seen. It took me a month of reading and practice to gain the confidence to shoot with it.

To get close enough with the Zeiss, I used a set of auxiliary close-up lenses that screwed on the front of the nonremovable 50 mm Zeiss lens. This camera served me well for many years; now, looking back, I think the Zeiss camera and close-up lens combination took pictures that were sharper than most that I take today. It was a sad day in the '70s when that camera finally gave up and died. No repairman could (or would) fix it.

My second camera, a Miranda Sensorex, offered the delightful luxury of interchangeable lenses and a built-in exposure meter. I used it for about a year and got great results. Then a friend, just out of the service, offered me a pair of Canon Pelixes with several lenses and lots of gadgets. This new gear was right off the boat from Vietnam — and the price was right.

The Canons and Sensorex performed well for several years until I eyed the new Nikon F, with its line of lenses. I sold the Sensorex and swapped the pair of Canons, lenses and all, for several model railroad kits and some much-needed cash.

During the same period I always had one or two viewfinder cameras. I am constantly experimenting. For instance, in the early 1970s I bought an Alpa 9d camera for its superb macro Switar lens. Nowadays I use the Alpa only for time exposures, because its shutter is worn and sluggish.

## ENVISIONING AND EXECUTING

There are basically three ways I produce model railroad photos.

One is to envision a complete picture with trains, props, and lighting. These "visions" can happen anytime. They're almost always mood shots, and usually based on a magazine photo, greeting card scene, or a story that I've been reading. I like to create photos that only exist in a land of make-believe.

Another way is to take pictures when the mood strikes, with no definite scene in mind. I will position the camera, add the train, focus, then take a couple of test shots. If the test results turn me on, I will dress the set by adding figures, autos, barrels, another tree or two, etc., until the picture pleases me. This method relies upon having a photogenic model railroad, one that will allow you to point the camera and shoot. Having a large model railroad and lots of props helps.

Both of these methods take hours for setup. Some-

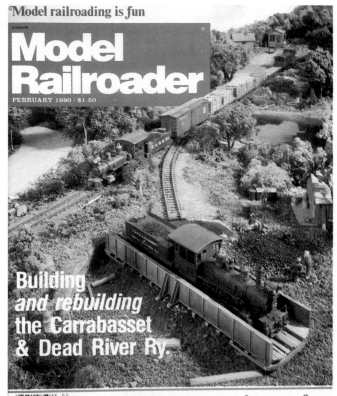

I always use a wide-angle lens for close-ups. It expands the perspective and gives the picture a "box Brownie" look. I like the elongation and distortion because it looks as if a scale person took the photo. A wide-angle lens also increases the apparent depth of field, so more of the scene is sharp.

A wide-angle lens takes a little getting used to. If you try to set up an eye-level shot, you'll see mostly the ceiling of the train room. This lens forces you to shoot down on the subject. By using the proper tilts on the view camera, you can increase the depth while correcting some of the distortion. It's about five feet from the front of the engine to the rear of this scene. It would be tough to get this kind of depth with a 35 mm camera and a 28 mm lens set at $f$ 22.

This shot was planned for a magazine cover. Cover shots require a vertical format and room in the top third of the picture for the magazine logo. The lighting is simple: Two main lights illuminate the whole train. I placed the lights to cast only one shadow. A diffused fill (close to the camera) lighted the near side of the engine.

times, after all this work, the test shots still don't pan out. Then I have to make a decision: Should I start over, or just rearrange things? Most of the time I will choose the latter course and stick with the shot until it pleases me.

Also, there are times when I've got a great idea but I can't pull it off technically. These shots usually involve multiple exposures, rear projection, or very low light levels. I'll usually keep shooting, even though I know I may only end up with one or two marginal pictures.

The third situation involves shooting a photo for hire. The client will call and describe a specific idea. I have to get the props (perhaps from an author or magazine), set the scene, and shoot it. Sometimes I don't get to see the finished photo until it's published. This forces me to be disciplined and deliver only what has been asked for.

Fig. 1. Here's what I carry in my Zero Halliburton case. I substituted a Ricoh for my second camera, a Nikkormat (which I used to take this picture).

## EQUIPMENT

When I leave the house for a shoot I carry three cases. In the first, a bulletproof Zero Halliburton, Fig. 1, I have an F-series Nikon camera body, a Nikkormat body, and my full array of lenses: 55 mm, f3.5, Micro-Nikkor P. C. macro lens; 35 mm, f2.8, Nikkor S wide-angle lens; 28 mm, f3.5, Nikkor wide-angle lens; and a set of 52 mm (thread size), +1, +2, and +3 close-up lenses (these screw on the front of the wide-angle lenses and act like magnifiers to allow the lenses to focus closer than normal). In addition, the case contains a Gossen Luna Pro exposure meter with a spot metering attachment, two Kodak 18 percent neutral gray cards with added color bars, a stopwatch, two cable releases, lens cleaning equipment, extra film, and a small (2½″ x 3½″ x 1¼″) electronic flash. The flash fires other flash units or adds fill light to an outdoor subject. This case is sturdy, yet small enough to fit under an airliner seat.

When I shoot products and small tabletop scenes I use a couple of Honeywell 204 Slave Strobonars, Fig. 2. These are "slaved" flashes (fired by a separate power source) and are balanced for 5500K daylight film. I put 30″ strings on the strobe mounting brackets to ensure the flashes are the same distance from the photo subject.

I also have a limited set of Cokin filters. These include a polarizer, a double-exposure matte box, a gradual blue No. 1, gradual blue No. 2, gradual gray No. 1, gradual gray No. 2, and a fog No. 1. I use the filters in situations where difficult or distracting backgrounds have to be modified or eliminated.

Magazine editors like a large image — it's easy to handle and evaluate. For this type of work I use a Calumet 4″ x 5″ view camera, Fig. 3. The 4″ x 5″ image is often close to the size of the published photo, meaning reproduction is sharp.

I usually put a 180 mm lens on the Calumet. After I learned to operate the camera, I bought a 90 mm wide-angle lens which has become my regular working lens.

In my second case is the Calumet with its dark cloth, a changing bag, 10 Graflex 4″ x 5″ film holders, a 90 mm wide-angle lens, a 180 mm normal lens, and a 127 mm lens (removed from an old Polaroid Model 110 and mounted on a 4″ x 5″ lens frame). I have a complete set of 3″ gel filters (along with their holders), lens shades, and adapter rings. Also in the case is a Polaroid 545 4″ x 5″ Land film holder, a Polaroid 405 Pack film holder, and a Horseman 4″ x 5″ exposure meter. I use the Polaroid 4″ x 5″ back mostly with Type 52 film (ASA 400) to evaluate exposure, judge lighting and composition, and for fast production shots. The Model 405 Pack film holder is used to produce quick black-and-white negatives with Polaroid's positive/negative black-and-white pack film.

The third box, a cardboard case, Fig. 4, contains three Acme-Lite 6″ bowl reflectors, lamp stands, and several spare 600-watt, 3200K DYH lamps (for tungsten film), along with extension cords, adapters, and fuses. I strap several Smith-Victor light stands and a Reflectasol 36″ umbrella to the side of the box, and pack a shoulder bag with odds and ends: film, model release forms, mirror, and a flashlight.

At home I use a 10″ Colortran Mini-Lite with barn doors and a 1000-watt, 3200K lamp. I also have several 10″ and 12″ bowl reflectors, each with its own diffuser, stand, and swiveling clamp. In these bowls I use 250-watt ECA 3200K lamps.

All my 35 mm color photos are on slide film. For indoor color photos, I like Kodak Ektachrome 50 Tungsten (EPY 135-36). For 35 mm daylight, I prefer Kodak Ektachrome 100 (EN 135-36). My two favorite 35 mm black-and-white films are Kodak Tri-X and Panatomic-X (FX 135-36). In the 4″ x 5″ view camera I use Kodak Ektachrome 6118 for transparencies, and Polaroid Polapan 52 for instant 4″ x 5″ black-and-white prints.

Commercial finishers develop my color film. However, I develop black-and-white photos at home in a small bathroom turned darkroom. I splurged and bought a Beseler 45MX II enlarger with several lenses, timers, etc. Window quilts darken the room, but I still have to do all the printing at night.

My advice is to learn how to use your present photo equipment before buying additional, more elaborate equipment.

Fig. 2. A Honeywell 204 Strobonar. This flash unit is balanced for 5500K daylight film.

Fig. 3. Large-format equipment: Calumet 4″ x 5″ view camera; two different Polaroid film backs; extra lenses and film holders; a film-changing bag; filters; and an extra cable release.

Fig. 4. For most field work, I use three portable Acme-Lite 600-watt (3200K) lamps in 6″ bowl reflectors.

It isn't often that the HOn2½ Carrabasset & Dead River Ry. gets a famous standard-gauge visitor. MODEL RAILROAD-ER Magazine celebrated its 50th anniversary in 1984 with a national tour of model railroads by an HO scale *Hiawatha*.

When it arrived on the C&DR I was ready. I had already set up the first scene (using an old engine as a stand-in), placed the lights, arranged the props, and had taken several Polaroid test exposures.

After I was sure I had captured a usable shot in both horizontal and vertical formats, I tried a third scene.

This is that third setup. I conceived it as a MODEL RAIL-ROADER cover, hoping either the first shot or this one would be used. The first shot was the one published.

The lighting varied from my standard practice: I used two main lights, front and back. The foreground main is a 500-watt lamp in a 12″ bowl placed above and to the left of the camera. It lit only the bottom half of the picture, so I positioned a second 500-watt main to illuminate the other half, matching the shadows of the two lights. I placed a 250-watt diffused fill above and to the right of the camera.

**DAVE FRARY 9**

(Left) Here in Winter Harbor on the C&DR, the pint-sized narrow-gauge engine meets the standard-gauge Maine Overland engine to swap goods and passengers.

This junction of two gauges is exactly the way that it used to be on the prototype. The narrow-gauge engines brought their trains to the interchange to swap freight and passengers. From this junction the standard-gauge trains continued south.

The "smoke" is painted on glass held in front of the camera. You can see from the set-up photo what a small area is actually photographed.

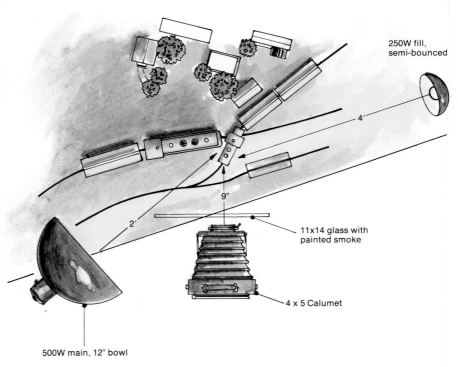

250W fill,
semi-bounced

4'

9"

2'

11x14 glass with
painted smoke

4 x 5 Calumet

500W main, 12" bowl

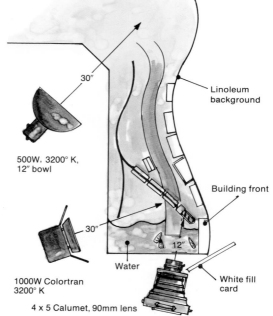

Linoleum
background

500W, 3200° K,
12" bowl

Building front

1000W Colortran
3200° K

Water

White fill
card

4 x 5 Calumet, 90mm lens

## COMPOSING AND SHOOTING A SCENE

The Polaroid snapshots above are test exposures; they show the sequence that created the finished photo.

I positioned the camera, added a few props, and took the first exposure to check the lighting. There was too much contrast, so I added a white fill card (a little to my right), which reflected a little more light to the shadowy areas along the front of the pier and on the sides of the buildings facing the camera.

Most of my locomotives were so big they blocked the view of the buildings and the street beyond the tracks. So I used my smallest piece of rolling stock, No. 29, a Joe Works industrial loco. I positioned it to fill one-third of the picture so it would become the center of interest.

The "rule of thirds" is a good way to establish a strong center of

interest in a photo. I draw imaginary lines to divide a scene into thirds, both horizontally and vertically. The intersection of the lines is a strong interest center that the viewer's eye will automatically go to. Use one interest center per picture.

I added more details — several figures, a second boat, two old trucks, and other items — and took the second exposure.

At this point I covered the camera, shut off the lights, and went to bed. I have found that it's always better to review a scene the next day when you're fresh, or when you have been away from the setup for several hours or even days. After studying the Polaroid shot for several minutes I decided that the scene needed to look busier. I added another boat (pointing toward the center of interest), moved the location of the rear truck so that it pointed at the engine, and added a fisherman on the dock. Satisfied with the scene, I made the final exposure, studied it, then shot color exposures with Ektachrome 6118 film.

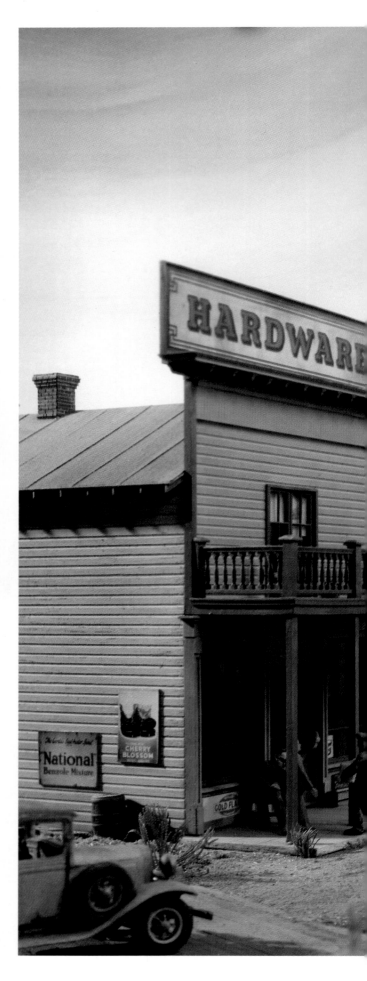

(Above) Renovation on the C&DR: I replaced most of the buildings and all of the larger trees with building facades arranged for the camera, and in progressively smaller scales to create a forced perspective. These "buildings" start at full HO scale (in the foreground) and continue to less than 2″ high in the rear. Full HO scale extends just past the diesel engine. The rear buildings are N scale and smaller; the farthest is only 20 inches from the camera.

I used the 35 mm Nikon with a 28 mm, f 3.5 lens at f 22, placed the camera, then added props, vehicles, and people.

Three lights illuminate the photo: a 1000-watt main, high and to the right of the camera; a diffused 250-watt fill, at camera height and to the left; and a 250-watt lamp, left rear, to provide even illumination of the backdrop.

(Right) As the old poem says, the mail must get through — and in the Maine woods, the railroad must move it. The mail is the reason engine No. 13 was fired up early on this fine autumn morning. Grover Hall, the Dead River hardware store proprietor, meets the train with the mailbag. If all goes on schedule the mail will be delivered by nightfall.

This scene was created for this photo. The hardware store rests on a 12″ x 12″ Styrofoam base. I mounted the diorama on a tripod and placed it against the edge of the layout so that the road areas matched. Trees, people, and vehicles complete the scene. For an early-morning look, I placed the main light low and to the left of the camera.

## FROM IMAGINATION TO IMAGE

(Left) I envisioned and planned this photo completely before I photographed it.

It started on a summer evening while I was looking through a book of train scenes. One picture caught my eye: It showed an engine in front of a station on a cold winter night. I looked at the photo for several minutes and said to myself, "If only there was a lighted Christmas tree in the station window." Suddenly, a vision of the scene etched itself in my mind.

I needed a lighted Christmas tree. After leafing through the Walthers catalog I decided there were no lamps available that were small enough. The next day I happened on a Radio Shack store having a sidewalk sale. In one of the bins of busted junk was a kit to build a fiber-optic lamp. Three dollars later I had the makings of my tree.

I cut a piece of styrene into the silhouette shape of a scale, seven-foot Christmas tree, and drilled about thirty holes (the same

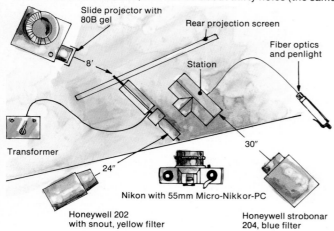

diameter as the fiber-optic ends) in the face of the tree. Each fiber-optic strand was fitted through a hole and glued into place. I glued a dime-sized, multicolored circle of acetate at the base of the fiber-optic bundle, then fitted the end of the bundle into a penlight with the lamp snug against the bundle. I put the tree in the front window of the station and fished the fiber-optics bundle out through the hole in the rear.

When the light shines through the colored acetate into the fiber ends, the color is transmitted throughout the fiber. Thus, each Christmas tree "bulb" shines a different color.

The set (a board with about 12" of N track mounted diagonally) is sprinkled with plaster-and-salt snow; the icicles are acetate. I taped a grain-of-wheat lamp inside the cab, and ran the wires to a transformer so I could adjust the lamp to match the intensity of the tree lights.

For the rear projection, I set the slide projector about eight feet behind a screen so the sky slide filled the camera's view. I had to angle the projection a little to get all corners of the projected slide in focus.

Because I planned to use Ektachrome 64 daylight film, I taped an 80B gel filter to the lens of the projector so its light would match the film's daylight color balance.

Two Honeywell strobes lighted the snow. The main (blue) light in the scene was a 204 Strobonar with a blue gel over the flash tube. The fill was a 202 Strobonar with a snout attachment and a yellow filter. The main flash was 30" above the scene and to the right; the fill flash was 24" to the left, level with the engine. Both flashes were set for high power output.

After many tests I made the final exposure as follows: I set the Nikon macro lens at f32, darkened the room, locked the shutter open, and manually fired both flashes. Next, I turned on the projector for five minutes to expose the background. Then I turned the engine cab light on for three minutes, and the tree lights for five minutes.

That's it — four separate exposures, totaling 13 minutes, on the same sheet of film.

This slide loses a lot of its impact when color separations are made for printing; the colors never quite look the same.

(Above) 'Tis the season for trains! Blue Ribbon Models was the original client, and MODEL RAILROADER used it, too. I used a Nikon with a Nikkor-S 35 mm lens stopped down to f16. Unlike most of my night scenes, this was a single exposure. I put 12-volt grain-of-wheat bulbs on variable transformers to balance the lighting. The main light (moonlight) was a microscope light with a blue gel taped over the lens.

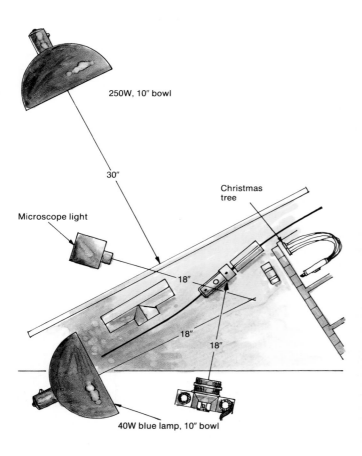

250W, 10″ bowl

30″

Christmas tree

Microscope light

18″

18″

18″

40W blue lamp, 10″ bowl

There's something special about a cold winter night, just after the snow has stopped falling. I am forever trying to get that feeling on a color slide.

This is my first night shot with an illuminated background. The method of illumination is explained fully in my book *How To Build Realistic Model Railroad Scenery* (Kalmbach). Briefly: I mounted a printed HO scale backdrop on a piece of frosted plastic, then cut out windows with an X-acto knife. I taped small swatches of colored gels behind the frosted plastic windows and lighted them with a floodlight (about 30″ behind the backdrop).

I lighted the foreground with a blue 40-watt lamp (in a bowl reflector) pointing straight down on the scene. This gives an overall blue to the shadows. The street lights are from an old Lionel train set; they are connected to a 12-volt transformer adjusted to about eight volts. The snowplow and flanger are lighted by a microscope lamp located above and slightly behind the backdrop. I controlled the light's coverage by taping black paper around the lamp to form a cone.

I used Kodachrome Type A (3400 degrees Kelvin) in a Nikkormat camera with a 35 mm lens. The exposure: blue light, five minutes; spotlight, 30 seconds; background light, one minute; street lights, 30 seconds; Christmas tree, five minutes.

Shots like this require accurate records and lots of test exposures. I combined the best of each test for the final shot.

(Above, left) I wanted to try out a new Cokin B1 gradual-blue filter. This filter is clear on the bottom half, and graduates to dark blue on the top half. It slides into a special holder that screws to the front of the lens so the filter can move up or down to place the blue exactly where you want it. I put the camera on a tripod, attached the filter, then mounted the glass in front of the lens.

The only problem in lighting the scene was a small reflection on the glass. I tried moving the fill light, but couldn't quite eliminate all of the reflection. A piece of semitransparent plastic between the light and the glass finally did the trick.

I added the smoke to the glass with a Q-tip dipped in Polly S flat white paint. I daubed the Q-tip on a piece of soft cloth to absorb most of the paint, then painted the glass. This has to be done while you are looking through the camera — great for the old hand-eye coordination!

(Left) This has to be my favorite shot. I set it up on a whim: I had just built the AHM plastic church, and I thought it would look good in a Christmas photo.

The church, the Fine Scale station, and the plastic AHM structure in the lower left are seated on a sheet of cardboard. I taped the grain-of-wheat bulbs in place to prevent them from moving during the exposure, then connected them to a single 12-volt train transformer and adjusted their intensity. I sprinkled flour "snow" over the scene with a large brush. The snowy hills in the background were cut from white paper.

There are two types of lights in this picture: the blue-filtered daylight from a strobe, and the warm, orange, tungsten light from the grain-of-wheat bulbs.

To take the photo, I opened the camera lens in the dark and fired the flash. Next, I turned on the grain-of-wheat lamps for about three minutes, then closed the camera lens. I repeated this procedure several dozen times, varying the amount of light from the grain-of-wheat bulbs. One of the two test rolls of film yielded six perfect exposures, each a little different from the others.

This small waterfront diorama depicts an old New England seed, feed, and grain storage facility that was located on tidal flats near my home.

I thought it would be interesting to try a photo on the base using buildings other than the feed mill. I placed the diorama base against a portion of the C&DR Ry. that had been removed for reconstruction, and put the background buildings on a board beside the base.

Because I wanted the main light to come from the rear of the scene, I put the 1000-watt Colortran at the rear about 4' from the right side of the camera. I used two 500-watt fills on either side of the camera, facing the scene and diffused with two large sheets of tracing paper.

The exposure is straightforward — no tricky techniques.

This is *the* basic photo: It's the only one in this chapter that is lit by sunlight and was shot with daylight film.

The sun provides enough light so that with fast film you can hold the camera in your hand, even at *f* 16, and get grab shots like this one. I turned the layout to find the best sun angle.

Most model railroaders are stuck in the attic or the cellar with immobile layouts. But if you have a portable pike or diorama base, by all means take it outside to photograph it! Have a friend hold a blue-sky background for you.

This photo was taken on the Elk River Railroad, a 3′ x 4′ portable HOn2½ layout. Photo courtesy of *Railroad Model Craftsman.*

To get the required depth in this photo on Bob Hayden's C&DR, I set the camera tilts and swings at the extremes, and the lens to the smallest *f*-stop. Strong backlighting illuminated the backdrop evenly. I set a diffused fill light next to the camera to soften the shadow cast by the bridge, and to add light to the front of the engine.

I had trouble with the contrast on this shot. This is the result of my third attempt.
I minimized the dark shadows by using the main almost as a backlight, placing it above and to the extreme left of the camera. For front light (to fill in the shadows) I used two diffused fill lights. One fill was directly above the camera, and the other was high and to the right. I put a sheet of tracing paper between the fill lamps and the subject to soften the light and illuminate the shadows.

(Right) It's tough when there's no room for the camera, lights, or photographer. On Bob's C&DR, I set the camera and rough-focused it before putting it in a narrow aisle. Due to the limited space, I mounted the key light on a small tripod on the layout (to the left of the camera). Only a good friend will let you set lights on his layout.

I've always liked the warm glow of incandescent lights contrasted against the dark of night, and I wanted to duplicate that phenomenon on film.

I placed two Honeywell strobes 18″ from the model. One was equipped with a snap-on blue filter, and illuminates the outside of the building. The other strobe had an orange filter and a fitted snout. The snout directs the light into the engine house. The filters and snout, plus a lot of other good stuff, are available in Honeywell's Strobonar accessory kit. I attached a flash cable to the camera and used a 55 mm macro lens. Three bracketed exposures produced the photo I wanted.

I was born in Salem, Massachusetts, in 1940, and grew up in the North Shore area north of Boston. I attended the University of Massachusetts on a football scholarship, and I've studied at several other colleges. I was a photographer for NASA for several years.

In collaboration with Bob Hayden, I have published over 1000 photos in MODEL RAILROADER, *Railroad Model Craftsman*, and other magazines, and have photographed and written product reviews and feature articles.

In 1980, I wrote a book about my scenery building techniques, *How To Build Realistic Model Railroad Scenery* (Kalmbach).

Until the summer of 1990 I worked for a public school system as a communications technician responsible for a TV studio, FM radio station, and repairing computers and audiovisual equipment. During warm summer and fall months I ran a small lobster business on the side. Now the lobster business is full-time.

I have two grown children who still think their old man is crazy for playing with trains.

(Left) This is the Franklin & South Manchester, an HO layout built by George Sellios. George's highly detailed layout is always a challenge to photograph, mainly because it soaks up a tremendous amount of light. I used four 1000-watt lamps and a long exposure just for a fairly simple shot like this one. George's layout was still growing when I shot it for MODEL RAILROADER Magazine's 1988 calendar — eventually it would be 16′ x 40′. And this was his first layout!

# Performing the art of illusion

## MALCOLM FURLOW

Model railroading and photography can draw you into a magical web of creativity and learning. I know — it happened to me!

My love affair with model photography began during the summer of 1978. Up until that time I was a professional musician traveling throughout the United States, playing Reno, Tahoe, Vegas, and a host of other, lesser-known watering holes.

As I look back on what seemed a strange transition at the time (becoming a photographer/modeler), I have now come to regard my entry into this creative field as a natural extension of my music career.

I still have a driving passion for music — but I feel fortunate to have added commercial photography and modeling to my experience as a musician. These are all steps in realizing my potential as a craftsman, artist, and individual.

You see, model railroading and photography, like music or any other art, come from the heart — each is a personal expression. My art reflects who I am.

Copying someone else's style just doesn't get it. Although an exchange of ideas is always helpful, an artist can't be successful if he is trying to emulate someone else, or change his own style to that of another.

In the case of model railroads, the ultimate creative vision is sometimes realized only after a prized model has been constructed, or a miniature scene fabricated and then photographed properly to complete the illusion. Model railroaders must surely benefit from a few carefully composed photos, especially if the layout or model has been lighted and photographed correctly.

For me, model railroading and photography have merged. Both incorporate fantasy and staging to present a compelling visual image — one that has personality or captures the illusion of life.

As you look through this book you must realize just how exciting model railroad photography can be, and what a great extension it can be to your own railroad modeling. I know that photographing model railroads led me to become a professional photographer, a field in which I actually had no prior interest!

---

A simple shot: an Sn3 diorama outdoors. I kept the fill card back from the set during this one-minute exposure to heighten contrast and better portray noontime light.

"Reunion at Bullhead Mine," on the S&T Ry. Here, I wanted to set up a situation with the train as a supporting actor. The actual subject is the two people hugging by the old car. The stack smoke, cylinder steam, and whistle exhaust are painted cotton that was moved during the exposure with a hair dryer set at low power.

## TRANSCENDING TECHNOLOGY

One of the most fascinating aspects of being "hooked" on model railroading is the art of illusion. I find producing an image on film miraculous in itself; when the art of photography is coupled with modeling, a true marriage of creativity and visual exploration is achieved.

Photographing models is seldom a chore. The effort that is required is usually well above and beyond that which I normally accord a commercial shooting session, yet I find it more fulfilling. Working with a precision instrument such as a camera and shooting a model scene that possesses the same level of accuracy is a joy — it feels right!

Oh yes, there's another tool that the authors of this book carry around with them: "visual literacy," the ability to see that which is to be registered on film. You might also call it "compositional forethought." It may take me half a day to shoot a photograph. But before loading the camera, I've spent at least that much time just *thinking* about the shot. With unlimited imagination we can reach as far as the boundaries of technology will allow.

(Left) Snakehead Gap on the Silverton & Telluride Railway. This picture says big mountains, small trains. The colorful engine works well against the subdued colors of the landscape. Although MODEL RAILROADER Magazine ran this shot on the cover, in many ways this is not a good cover shot because it encompasses so much detail. Cover photos are less busy so the magazine's information can be added without the whole thing looking cluttered.

## WHAT THE FUTURE HOLDS

Polaroid pioneer Dr. Edwin Land once said, "Nothing you can imagine is technology unfeasible." If we gaze into our crystal ball for a moment, we can see things that are almost magical.

Imagine! How about an all-purpose film, one that could "self-develop," much as Polaroid has for years, but with the added dimension of providing prints or transparencies either in black-and-white or color, and in perfect, faithful color — without artificial light or chemical imagery!

Or, a wallet-size camera that could perform alongside today's workhorses, but without having to switch lenses or calculate exposure. Fully automatic, this camera will free the photographer to exercise artistic expression unfettered by technical bonds. Are we talking about a computerized camera? I think so.

All of these advances in automatic control will require a more potent power supply, one that would far outdistance present batteries.

Then, mechanical moving parts will be eliminated in favor of total electronic control, and lenses will become more flexible — like macro lenses, but smaller, lighter, and integrated into the body of the "super camera."

These are only some of the changes that are sure to come as science marches on. While thumbing through one of Kodak's workshop-series books, I noted a sentence that sums it up: "There is a saying among inventors that the man who says something cannot be done is likely to be interrupted by the man who has just done it." I wish I had said that!

(Above) Fig. 1. Clockwise from the stopwatch: wide-angle lens; Polaroid film back for test shots; below that, a couple of 4″ x 5″ film holders; Linhof camera (4″ x 5″ format); Mamiya camera (6 cm x 7 cm format); lens for the Mamiya with large hood attached; a Polaroid film back adapted to the Mamiya 6 cm x 7 cm; a shutter-release cable; a filter holder; a flash meter; another film back, with adapter attached.

## EQUIPMENT

My arsenal of photographic gear centers around the quest for greater depth of field. Medium- to large-format cameras produce the most desirable image, given the problems of photographing miniatures.

However, the equipment needed for taking good model railroad photos is fairly modest. Consider these five main points:
- Depth of field
- Focus
- Composition
- Film choice
- Lighting

My Linhof camera (4″ x 5″ format) produces wonderful results — especially for depth of field — while at the same time reducing grain. The Linhof's large-format negative stands up well when it's enlarged. I use it for all my color cover work, even though it is bulky, time-consuming, and requires sheet film.

A big advantage with this camera is its ability to effect (or correct) distortion, especially with a wide-angle lens (like a 90 mm Super-Angulon). The Linhof accepts a Polaroid back, allowing me to check exposure and composition before using "real" film.

I also use a dilapidated Mamiya RB67 medium-format camera. This camera has interchangeable backs (I load one with black-and-white, the other color), and takes a Polaroid back, too. The Mamiya is more mobile than the Linhof, although I normally use the Mamiya on a tripod. Both cameras allow double exposures.

My third camera is a Pentax Spotmatic 35 mm, used mostly for wide-angle shots.

I'm not much for using photofloods, as the quality of light can suffer after repeated use. Quartz lamps work better, live longer, and are easier to pack and maintain. I use three Smith-Victor lights: a couple of 1,000-watt model 750s and a 650-watt. If I have to photograph a large layout, I use more 1,000-watt lights — up to six of them if I have an adequate power supply. I also use flash equipment, but merely to augment (rather than being the prime source of) illumination.

I carry color-correction filters as well as polarizers and special-effect filters. They are all gel-type filters (rather than screw mounts). I carry filters for my flash gear, especially if I want to balance tungsten lights with flash.

My Minolta Model III flash meter reads either ambient or direct light. This thing is great — digital readout, reads flash with or without a cord input, and is usually dead accurate.

I use at least two Reflectasol umbrellas for fill lighting. I seldom use fill cards because I've gotten accustomed to using the umbrellas.

A 4″ x 5″-format camera requires sheet film such as Kodak 6118 Tungsten (ASA 50), or Ektachrome 64 for daylight. I use the same ASA emulsion for 6 cm x 7 cm film. However, for some shots I use Kodachrome high-speed film that is rated at ASA 160. For 35 mm photography, I use either ASA 160 Tungsten, ASA 40 Kodachrome, or ASA 64 Kodachrome that is formulated for daylight. Whatever the format, Plus-X Pan works well for black-and-white shots.

(Above) Fig. 2. Lighting: I use three Smith-Victor quartz lamps (with barn doors to aim the light) like the one on the left; two smaller quartz lamps (middle); and two flash heads with slaves (bottom). For fill lighting, I use the umbrella to reflect or "bounce" light; this indirect lighting is softer and balances shadowy areas.

## 34 MALCOLM FURLOW

Witness a classic example of why the Linhof camera works well for photographing models. I wanted the locomotive on Lorrel Joiner's O scale layout to jump out at the viewer. So I positioned the camera about 12″ from the front of the loco.

Depth of field would be a problem were it not for a camera that can "swing and tilt," correcting perspective by changing the alignment of the lens and film boards. I achieved good depth of field over a 25-foot layout span. The first exposure was for a minute at *f*8; the second exposure, two minutes at *f*64. I used a 90 mm wide-angle lens.

(Above, left) I used a 35 mm camera to document a typical lighting setup in my upstairs studio. The layout is an Sn3 module with a brass shay from Milestone Models (courtesy of Bill Peter). The main, or key, light is slightly behind the model for backlighting. This gives a nice glow to the tops of locomotive cabs and domes, and adds dimension and depth to the photo. The fill light (650-watt) is about eight feet away from the engine, at about the same angle as the camera.

(Right) I wanted this photo to look three-dimensional without revealing the mirror positioned in the far corner. Spotlighting the "Galloping Goose" sitting on the turntable gave a nice glow to the curved roof of the rail bus. The exposure: *f*64 for two minutes using a magenta color correction filter (cc10m).

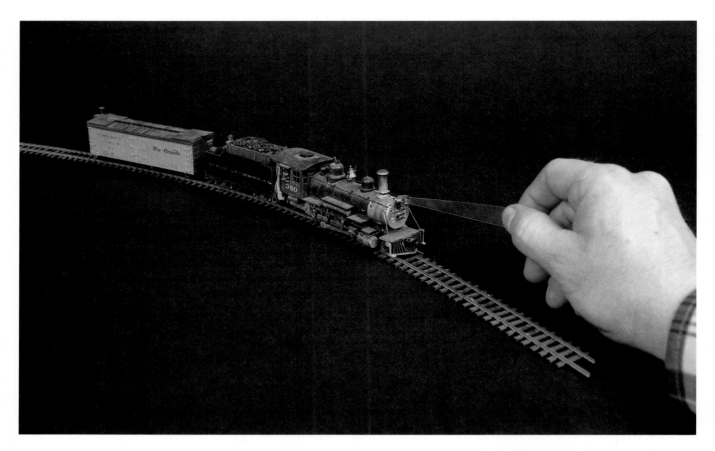

Here's how to replicate a traveling headlight beam. Place a piece of clear plastic or a clear soda straw against the headlight. "Burn in" the loco headlight with the floods off and the soda straw in place. Remove the straw and take a second exposure with the floods turned on.

(Above) It's the old cotton smoke trick. One end of the painted cotton is inserted in the smokestack of the locomotive. A thin, black wire is attached to the other end of the cotton. Moving the cotton during an exposure of 15 seconds or more produces billows of "smoke" in the photo.

(Right) "Winter at Coots Gap." Two exposures were necessary for this shot. I attached a clear plastic straw to the engine headlight and shot the first exposure at *f*8 for two minutes.

Then I closed the shutter and turned on the photo floods. After removing the straw and taping a blue filter over the lens, I took the second exposure at *f*64 for four minutes.

**38 MALCOLM FURLOW**

When the *Hiawatha* toured the nation to celebrate MODEL RAILROADER Magazine's 50th anniversary, she traveled way out west to the Denver & Rio Chama Western (left) and way on down to San Antonio (above), where she spent a night at the Great Southern passenger station in the heart of the city.

Lorrel Joiner's Great Southern is a famous O scale layout, and with good reason: It's housed in its own 50′ x 60′ building in his backyard!

In the shot at left, large scale figures placed close to the camera (2″) created a forced perspective. The first exposure was for one minute at *f* 64, during which I wiggled cotton over the loco smokestack. During the second exposure (one minute at *f* 64), I slowly waved cotton over the cab.

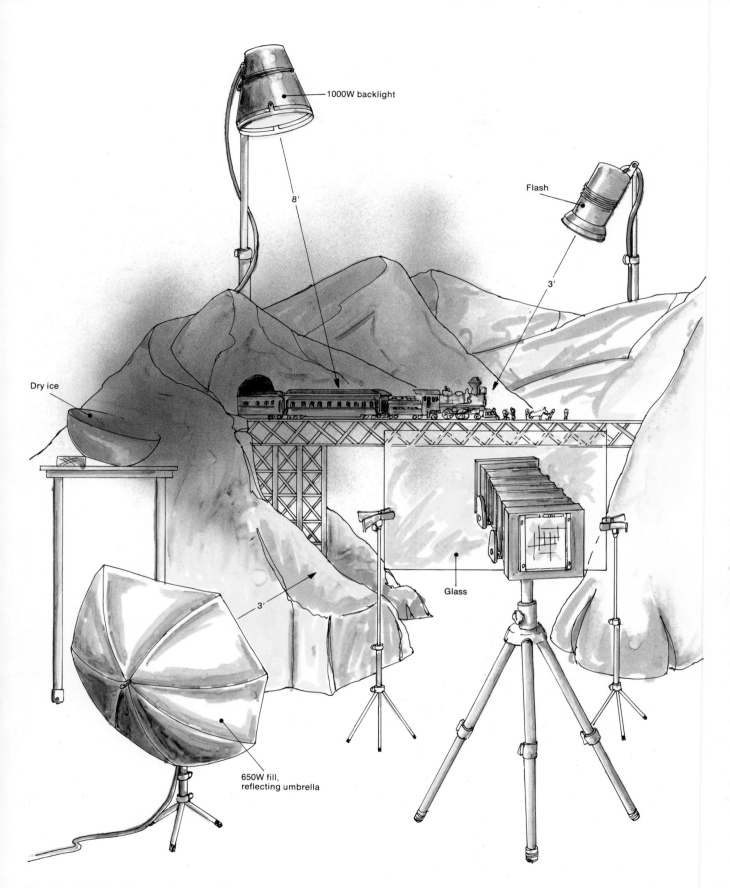

1000W backlight

8'

Flash

3'

Dry ice

3'

Glass

650W fill,
reflecting umbrella

**Whoa mule! This shot required three exposures.**

I wanted the fog effect to be subtle, to avoid distracting from the scene. Many of the effects, such as the coach light (front window) and the lantern, are painted on glass held between the scene and the camera. The glow from the cab (simulating an open firebox door) is a combination of small bulbs and painted glass. The fog is partly painted on glass, partly dry-ice fog blown into the scene.

The first exposure, to burn in the headlight and coach lights, was for one minute at ƒ11. During the second exposure (one minute at ƒ64) I used cotton to create engine smoke and cylinder steam. I positioned the painted glass and fired the flash (to freeze the fog) during the third exposure (three minutes at ƒ64).

Mike and Barbara Sigmon helped me by providing the extra sets of hands needed while shooting this photo.

(Above) A fog shot in progress (for a late evening or early morning scene). Along with the tungsten lights, a flash must be used (with a corrective filter taped over the lens) to freeze the motion of the fog. That's me on the right; my friend Billy Haynes is holding the flash. The photo was taken by Scott Dorset.

(Left) This shot employed some difficult techniques, and three exposures. The first exposure (for the headlight and passenger car light) was for 15 seconds at f 5.6.

The second exposure: 45 seconds at f 32 with the floodlights.

For the third exposure, I removed the cotton from the stack, blew "fog" (dry ice) into the scene, and froze the motion of the fog with an electronic flash. Two meters were used: one to measure ambient light, the other a flash meter.

Metered calculations for both ambient light and flash require the floods to be two stops "hotter" than the flash; the latter freezes the movement of the fog with just enough light to make the fog visible.

The dry-ice effect will not work with just floodlights because the exposure (one minute total) would be too long. The fog is moving through the scene, which would make it invisible during a long exposure.

(Next page) I had a great time building this photo set. I invited my friends and their kids to a party and asked them to dress in period clothing, then went around the party and shot Polaroid photos of everyone. I even used myself — cheap model! That's Paul Scoles with yours truly at the crossing. Cutouts must be perpendicular to your line of sight so the edges are not seen. Also, they have to be placed far enough away from the lens to blend into the scenery. A few model-railroad purists were miffed when MODEL RAILROADER Magazine ran these shots, but I readily admit this is more photography than modeling. And it's fun!

(Above) Obviously, this must be an advertising shot for Kodak. This four-minute exposure on my D&RC uses valance lighting with 250-watt bulbs. For the fill light, I bounced a 650-watt Smith-Victor light from a 4′ Reflectasol umbrella. The figures are held in place with rubber cement.

(Right) A typical shoot on the D&RC. The 4″ x 5″ sheet film is loaded into a holder in the back of the camera. The dark slide is then removed and the photo taken. Note that my 4″ x 5″ camera requires a heavy-duty tripod.

(Left) A scene from Vic Butterworth's N scale Enport, Rogue River & Thataway Ry. Notice how the lower train draws you into the picture. I was impressed with Vic's modeling. Working on a small budget, he turned a small space into an interesting place with ingenious building and artistic talent.

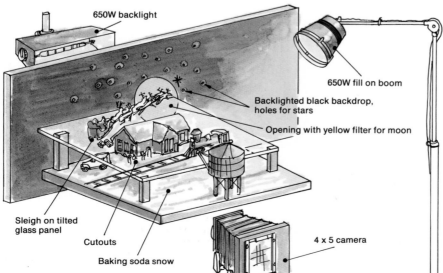

650W backlight

650W fill on boom

Backlighted black backdrop,
holes for stars

Opening with yellow filter for moon

Sleigh on tilted
glass panel

Cutouts

Baking soda snow

4 x 5 camera

"Christmas Eve at Soda Springs Depot." Many people associate trains with Christmas. I wanted some childish magic in this shot.

The biggest task in this shot was collecting all the props. The snow is baking soda, the people are cutouts. A glass panel, tilted a little, holds Santa aloft. The sky is a backdrop with holes punched in it, backlighted. For the moon, I fitted an opening in the backdrop with a yellow filter.

I used the Linhof with 6118 tungsten film. The first exposure (two minutes at f 16) burned in the moon and stars. For the second exposure (one minute at f 64), I turned on the 650-watt fill and created the smoke effects over the loco and the depot.

"Season's Greetings From Days Past." I put an 11″ x 14″ piece of glass in front of the lens and flicked white paint on it to simulate falling snow. The windowpane is made of wood molding; plastic snow and backwards lettering complete the foreground. The engine exhaust is darkened cotton, moved during the two-minute exposure.

SILVER canyon
on the D&RGWRR
M Furlow Denver
1891

The charms in this shot are the sepia tone and the writing, both done during the printing step in the darkroom. The words were printed on an 11″ x 14″ sheet of glass placed over a sheet of photo paper and exposed. The ink on the glass prevented light from passing through the letters; thus, the writing shows up white, like an old glass-plate negative. When I shot the photo, I left the area where I knew the writing would appear somewhat dark to ensure good contrast.

(Left) An "S" curve is always a strong compositional element. I allowed the framing to fall hard to the right to let the scenery enhance the shot and help support the leading players in this picture — the engine and the train. Thoughtful composition helps reinforce the perception that the train is actually moving through the scene.

(Above) Goin' up Cripple Creek on Jim Rubado's On3 scale Tomahawk & Lobo Creek RR. Depth and panoramic views are required to capture the Colorado Rockies scenery of Jim's railroad. Utilizing the swings and tilts of the Linhof 4″ x 5″ camera and shooting with the Angulon 90 mm wide-angle lens also increased the depth and scope of the photo.

(Right) I like this shot a lot, but I'm even more proud of my modeling in this scene: I think it's some of my best work. Model details become crucial in a large scale like this G scale Soda Creek & South Park Ry. Stock figures didn't look realistic to me, so I used a real person — a photo of him, that is. The fireman in the window is a Polaroid photo of my next door neighbor. I made a print from a transparency of the scene, placed the cutout photo on the print, retouched it a bit, then photographed the composite on 4″ x 5″ film.

**54 MALCOLM FURLOW**

**MALCOLM FURLOW 55**

(Above) Paul Scoles and I teamed on this shoot of Ken Davis' HO scale Great Northland Ry. Ken's railroad is under a low ceiling, making it hard to get to. The bay scene on the backdrop provided a nice feeling of depth. Raising the camera seemed to "expand" the picture, as did the leading lines of the two tracks and the train.

(Left) Here's a good example of how you can compose the elements of a picture to lead the viewer's eye through the scene to the center of interest. Notice how various "miscellaneous" items in the frame — the logs and the truck in the foreground, the telephone poles, the lines in the rockwork — all point toward the center of the photo. The speeding train in the background is an easy trick that animates this scene. During the exposure I slowly pulled the train backwards as smoothly as I could.

I built my first layout back in 1978 — the HOn3 Denver & Rio Chama Western. Photos and construction techniques of the Rio Chama have appeared in most of the major modeling publications in the U.S., and overseas, too. The D&RCW appeared in Kalmbach's video "Weathering Railroad Models With Malcolm Furlow" and The Imagination Station video "Expanding the Denver & Rio Chama Western with Malcolm Furlow." An article for Kodak's workshop series (KW22) included scenes from the Rio Chama as well as other layouts that I have photographed for MODEL RAILROADER Magazine.

Another project, building the HOn3 San Juan Central layout for MODEL RAILROADER, was a heavyweight undertaking which culminated in a book called *HO Narrow Gauge Railroad You Can Build* (Kalmbach).

Strange how easily creativity leads from one art form to another. From music to model railroading to photography to a video production company to . . . a career in Western art! I got my start painting backgrounds for my model railroads, and I guess the foreground switched from three- to two-dimensional. I've had a fair amount of success at it: My work appears in galleries all over the world, and hangs in such noble homes as those of Samuel Goldwyn and President George Bush.

However, I haven't given up model railroading. I've been working on what might eventually be the world's largest layout, a Rio Chama of mucho grande proportions in the lobby of the Children's Medical Center at Parkland Memorial Hospital in Dallas. How big is this layout? At this writing, 75' x 35' and two stories tall — a stairway passes through one of its canyons! The kids receive a boarding pass and an engineer's cap, they can watch the trains from their rooms on closed-circuit television, and there's even a spot on the layout where they can operate some of the trains! I'm especially proud of this project.

**A Galloping Goose on the loose on the San Juan Central. This shot is based on a prototype photo of a Rio Grande Southern Goose shaking across a spindly trestle in southwestern Colorado. The low camera angle gives the viewer the illusion of being in a canyon. Strong, high-contrast lighting replicates mountain sunlight.**

**MALCOLM FURLOW 59**

# The realities of fantasy

## JOHN OLSON

The public has a misconception about model railroaders. We're seen as funny little fat men with striped engineers' caps, running around with badges and doing nothing but playing with trains. I'm here to tell you lots of us enjoy more or less normal pursuits, too.

Most of what I have learned about model railroads and cameras has been through seeing photographs. Still, I rate photography second to my enjoyment of model railroading. My continued interest in the photographic aspect of model railroading is surprising to me. Certainly one doesn't automatically lead to the other. Yet, here I am, film in hand, calculating exposures.

When I started photographing model railroads, I made exposures from all possible viewing angles — and one in ten was usable. Even if they were all good exposures — usable for documentation, maybe — only that one in ten effectively communicated my message (statement) in the scene.

Probably all photographers go through similar growing pains, but once past that stage and upon looking back you'll have developed a sense of composition and statement.

---

This photo on the Jerome & Southwestern appeared in my book entitled *Building An HO Model Railroad With Personality* (Kalmbach).

The idea was to create the broad, expansive vista of a desert scene in a small (4' x 8') railroad area. To achieve this, I used a 2¼"-format camera at ƒ90 with a wide-angle lens. I knew I needed a horizontal format, but I adjusted the height of the camera several times before I captured the scene I was after.

To get the brightness of the desert, I saturated the scene with even lighting, balancing the actual scenery with the printed backdrop. I placed the main light that was nearest the camera directly over the caboose to accent window frames, grab irons, etc., being careful not to over-illuminate the side of the caboose and flatten out the scene.

The train's curving position further expresses the expansiveness of the overall scene and helps tie the foreground and background together.

The beautiful backdrop is a water-color by Tom Daniel. I wanted to use sunlight to let the colors really pop! However, I had to be careful of how much sunlight was introduced by the reflecting card (to maintain the light balance between the three-dimensional model and two-dimensional backdrop; you can see a little of the card off to the side in the setup shot). So I took several exposures, with the card filtered slightly more each time. I didn't know which one would work until I saw the developed film.

Notice in the setup shot how I used foam rubber, a backdrop, a bounce card, and anything else I could find to prop up this model. The whole setup sat on a rubber trash can!

## LIGHTS, CAMERA — FRENZY!

Without purpose, no photo can be effective. The critical first step in setting up a scene — setting up my bracketing, exposure, and all — is to take the camera in hand and look at everything as though I were a cyclops, a one-eyed (like the camera) giant. I walk around the scene, moving up and down, side to side, in and out, throwing focus and looking for the elements that give the scene character, balance, and depth of field.

During a typical exposure you'll find my friend Ron Dickson and me running around behind the camera, tripping and stumbling and running for odds and ends. I might simulate smoke by jiggling a piece of black thread. Meanwhile, Ron's got a hand over one of the lights, trying to dodge one roof that's a little too

bright. In my other hand I've got a piece of gel, trying to get a little blue into the shadow for a feeling of coolness, or I'm picking up the flashlight and trying to open those areas underneath the carriage of the locomotive where all the light doesn't bounce in as it should. Meanwhile, somebody is still trying to keep track of how far we are through our one-minute exposure. So any one of these exposures is quite a carnival, and no two of them come out alike because there's so much spontaneity.

The predominant problem in shooting photos of a model railroad is making sure everything is where it belongs. For example, I'll spend hours taking three or four exposures, getting everything properly balanced and the lights set. Then I get the pictures back, project them, take a look and oops! one of the little scale men tipped over and he's in the ditch upside

I calculated the focus in this scene for the man on the boxcar roof. The figure running toward the camera (left foreground) is intentionally blurred, but to aid the illusion no foreground objects — sharp-edged crates, cars, or wharf junk — were included. Such items would have made the photo look technically poor.

The main light is pointed toward the lens of the camera, so I used a cardboard baffle on the light to prevent glare.

I used the Yashica twin-lens camera with a wide-angle lens. Vignetting (a reduction of illumination at the edges of the picture) occurs when the camera has the wide-angle lens and is focused 36″ or more away. I compensated by taking "more" photo than I wanted, then cropping the print. Placing the twin-lens Yashica 24 right on the layout and composing through the top-mounted viewfinder outweighs any problems caused by vignetting.

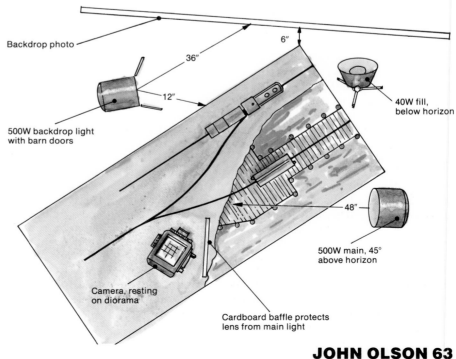

Backdrop photo

6″

36″

12″

40W fill, below horizon

500W backdrop light with barn doors

48″

500W main, 45° above horizon

Camera, resting on diorama

Cardboard baffle protects lens from main light

**JOHN OLSON 63**

Here's one of my early efforts (1976). To depict the deep shadows of late afternoon in the High Sierras, I positioned a single 250-watt light source at a low angle close to the rear of the scene. I used a white bounce card to light the shadowy areas on the sides of the buildings and the loco. The length of the exposure allowed me to manipulate the card to direct light throughout the scene as needed.

down or a tree is cockeyed or I've got a telephone pole coming out of the top of the locomotive. These are little frustrations, but they can ruin a photo and I have to take time to look for them.

## DEPTH OF FIELD

I work mainly with two kinds of depth of field, although one of them I use less these days — what I call the infinite depth of field.

People think that when you scale yourself down to shooting model scenes (as though you were there as a real person in that model) that you need an infinite depth of field, that everything from your toes ad infinitum should be in focus.

That doesn't happen in the real world. Our vision has falloff — the near ground is out of focus, the far ground is out of focus. In fact, the far ground is a little soft on even a normal (full-size) exposure. So I try to stay away from those ƒ 128, three-hour exposures where the whole picture is so sharp you can cut your finger on it, and go for something more in what would be the ƒ 8 range in real-world photography. There is a little falseness — a little softness in the foreground, a little bit in the background. Just like a portrait, the focus is slightly soft. You fall into a more normal perspective, and I think you get a more realistic picture.

## VISIONS AND FANTASIES

The goal in my photographs is to bring people into a world that doesn't really exist except through my eyes — through my experience. You can enter another dimension, a miniature world. I'm not as interested in scale model accuracy as in sharing my visions and fantasies with other people. Through my camera I'm able to bring them to my world, and I think that speaks for my style.

My photos are intended to capture the look and feel of a visit to my railroad. I work hard to exclude peripheral items from the camera's eye (edge of the railroad, control panels, etc.) because these are distractions. However, I hope to avoid technical stunts that would portray my model railroad differently from how it actually looks. I don't confuse creative photography with ingenious special-effects photography.

Any changes I have made in my techniques have been to communicate better. However, there have been such revolutionary developments in photography that photojournalists will soon be able to create a scale world that goes far beyond the limits of the actual model. High-tech camera, video, and print processes can make average models look extraordinary. This is *Star Wars* stuff, heavy on the special effects — not wrong, just not my direction.

## 64 JOHN OLSON

The shots at the bottom of this page show the effects of different exposures. Note how the exposure affects not only the picture's ambience but also the visibility of certain details.

This scene was staged on the front edge of my HOn3 Mescal Lines Railroad. To add depth to the scene and to frame the photo, I added a large pine tree (in a block of plastic foam sitting on a stool) just in front of the camera. I kept the tree in shadow so it wouldn't detract from the center of interest, and to reinforce the right-to-left flow of the scene, ending at the locomotive's headlamp. Since this was to be a magazine cover, I wanted the focal point (the headlamp) to be directly under the magazine logo. I rotated the camera to get the vertical format needed for a cover shot.

Because I positioned the 500-watt main light above and behind the camera, little fill light was required to balance the exposure for the intense High Sierra lighting I was after.

Normally, having the main light directly behind the camera yields a flat lighting effect. For impact and balance it was proper here, because a magazine cover will have a logo and other graphics in addition to the photo. Therefore, it was important that the main center of interest be clear.

(Above) **Fig. 1. I use these lenses for almost all my work.**

(Right) **Fig. 2. The Argus Argoflex camera and an assortment of pinhole apertures. I modified this camera permanently for pinhole use.**

## EQUIPMENT

My equipment revolves around two different kinds of cameras, a 2¼"-square-format twin-lens reflex camera, and a 35 mm single-lens reflex. The square-format camera gives me a large negative, better resolution, and lets me get right down on the model surface with the taking lens. I like the single-lens reflex camera because of the interchangeable lenses.

The three lenses in Fig. 1 perform 99 percent of my focusing duty. On the left is the Vivitar Series One 70-210 mm, 1:35 macro-focusing zoom. I use this lens to compress a scene — a feature of all long focal-length lenses — and to highlight a subject by throwing foreground and background out of focus (due to the short depth of field inherent in long lenses). I use this lens

rarely — perhaps 10 percent of the time.

The middle lens is a Vivitar Series One 24-48 mm, 1:38 auto zoom. Wide-angle lenses have great depth of field and create a feeling of vastness. When used at f 22 (my preference), entire scenes are in focus. The 24 mm setting allows me to get into tight aisles and still capture a broad view. I use this lens 30 percent of the time.

On the right is a Nikon Micro-Nikkor P·C Auto 1:3.5, 55 mm lens. This box of glass provides razor-sharp focusing, and its f 32 maintains depth of field even up close. It focuses 9 inches from the subject, allowing 1:2 or ½ actual-size images — great for loco details like drivers, valve gear, etc. I use this lens the most.

The Nikkormat EL camera is my workhorse. Its onboard metering is accurate and reliable, with shutter speeds of 4 to ¹/₁₀₀₀ seconds. At least half of my work requires

speeds using the "B" setting — more than 4 seconds of open shutter — and in this manual (with cable release) setting, the meter remains on. I can observe lighting changes as they occur.

I also use a Nikon FE2, which is essentially a refined and evolved Nikkormat EL. However, the Nikon has the advantage of an 8-second to ¹/₄₀₀₀-second range, and a double-exposure lever. Double exposure is exciting because a photo can be exposed and compiled element by element.

The reason for two cameras is to have color film in one and black-and-white in the other, so I can shoot the same scene without changing film.

Some years ago Paul Scoles and I began experimenting with pinhole cameras: ultra-small apertures to increase the depth of field, or even achieve lens-to-infinity focus. It's a way to aim at the locomotive and have

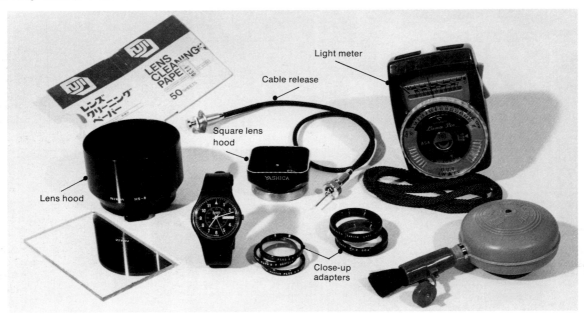

Light meter

Cable release

Square lens hood

Lens hood

Close-up adapters

**Fig. 4. Common accessories. The close-up adapters provide focusing options for the Yashica camera.**

Fig. 3. The Yashica is a twin-lens reflex camera. Here you see it fitted with a wide-angle lens, great for close-up work.

Fig. 5. My usual array of lights. The adjustable barn doors on the Colortran (bottom left) allow me to direct this high-intensity light accurately.

the caboose remain in crisp focus. Any camera can be adapted, though we chose 2¼″ twin-lens cameras because of the large-format negative and (more important for us) relatively low prices of used twin-lens cameras. Originally, I fitted a Yashica-24 camera with an iris made of .005″ brass sheet, and obtained an effective *f*-stop of 128. The Yashica had a few other features that I wanted — attachable lenses, close-up and wide-angle lenses, filters, cable release, self timer, and so on.

However, installing the pinhole disk on the iris of the camera prevented me from using all those options. So I bought a secondhand (and much simpler) Argus Argoflex twin-lens camera for permanent dedication to pinhole use, Fig. 2.

Figure 3 shows the Yashica as I typically use it, with a wide-angle lens. The bayonet lens mounts are so easy to use that changing focus and depth of field with close-up attachments is never a fuss. The wide-angle lens changes the normal 80 mm permanent lens to an approximate 58 mm wide-angle. This increases the picture area by about 75 percent and increases the depth of field. I modified the wide-angle lens by adding a Series Five close-up lens.

When composing and focusing an exposure I attach this hybrid lens to the upper (or viewing) lens, focus, then move it to the lower (or taking) lens and raise the camera the distance between the center of each lens.

Figure 4 shows the auxiliary items I use most frequently. Let's move clockwise, beginning with the lens-cleaning paper. Next is the square lens hood for normal (all but the wide-angle) lenses of the Yashica. It shields the taking lens from stray light. The cable release has a locking feature to hold the shutter open as long as five minutes. I use a Gossen Luna-Pro hand-held meter to double-check all camera meter readings and for metering unusual conditions. The squeeze bulb and brush are for lens and camera cleaning. The two stacks of rings are close-up adapters for the Yashica. They provide an increased range of focusing op-

tions. Note that my watch has a second hand: Reliable, easy-to-read second and minute hands are required. The mirror is really a small piece of mirrored Plexiglas used to bounce light into shadowy areas. Finally, we come to the lens hood I use on all 52 mm-diameter lenses for my 35 mm cameras.

All my lights use 3200K lamps, from 40 to 500 watts (and rarely, 1000). Usually, the main is 500 watts, fill 100-250 watts, and backlight 100 watts. On the Colortran light, Fig. 5, the barn doors are required when high-intensity 500- and 1000-watt lamps are used. Above the Colortran in Fig. 5 is a common photoflood, used for fill and backlighting: Some models have wattage limits — be sure not to exceed them. To the right of the flood is an incandescent, single-bulb, swing-arm drafting lamp. I use

Luxo L-1s with bulbs between 40 and 100 watts. This light is great because it can be clamped and pointed almost anywhere. Finally, a flashlight. I use it for painting light into hard-to-light areas. Typically, during a 10-second exposure I will use it for 2 to 6 seconds, keeping it moving to avoid hard-edged shadows or over-illumination. This technique takes practice — it's a seat-of-the-pants operation.

Every once in a while a setup requires special help, Fig. 6. This little light is a Mole-Richardson Mini-Mole. It has all sorts of attachments, some of which are shown: focusing lenses, snoots, gels (for colored light), and ring holders for the flimsy gels.

A tripod is necessary whenever the shutter speed is less than ¹/₆₀. A good one should be easily adjustable for height, angle, and tilt, and should lock securely.

Fig. 6. I use the Mini-Mole to fine-tune lighting. Its accurate aim and color attachments let me selectively light a single element in a scene.

The Christmas tree in the town park, people hustling about, and the arrival of the train all contribute to the holiday mood of this photo. The color shot has no background, which helps to focus attention. The black-and-white shot uses a blackout background to achieve the same goal, and is shot from a more natural viewing angle.

The lighting was touchy for this scene. The snow was so reflective that slight changes in the camera settings made great changes in the exposure. I had to recalculate the exposure for every shot. I attached a hood to the lens (about 1″ deep) to avoid flares.

Taco Bell was the client for this photo, and the color in its printed version was intentionally exaggerated by shifting heavily to magenta and cyan to pump up the holiday, toy-like feeling. I used fluorescent lights to give a slight blue cast to shadowy areas. The printing magnified the effect.

Note how the camera angle (and thus, the format) is different for a magazine cover. A steep angle on this shot produces a more vertical shot and leaves more background at the top of the frame, a good place to put the magazine title and logo.

**68 JOHN OLSON**

I used a wide-angle lens, placed near the water surface and looking up at a steep angle, to emphasize verticality in this scene. The ripples in the cast-resin surface make the water appear to be in motion. Hand painting "white water" with acrylics helped augment the effect.

There is a bridge, just out of the scene at the top, that was difficult to shoot around, and in trying to avoid it I arrived at this angle. I chose to frame the scene by keeping the rock bluff in the right foreground in shadow, spilling just enough light on the bluff for it to be legitimate.

The high angle of main lighting also accents the vertical thrust of the mine dock pilings and gives a sense of warmth to the scenery.

The steep canyon walls, water, and high sky (coupled with the upward focus of the viewing angle) are essential in this rugged Eastern Sierra scene.

(Next page) For "A Day at Mule Shoes Meadow" (April 1976 MODEL RAILROADER Magazine), I needed a variety of backdrops to reflect the changing light of an evolving dayscape. Since I'm not a background painter, I experimented with rear-projected slides that I had photographed while on research trips. I began the setup by positioning the projector and screen to be in scale with the three-dimensional model. Since the projector operates at a fixed intensity (having no variables), I balanced the model lights to the rear-projection screen. I used daylight film, so an 80A correction filter was necessary. Experimenting with the camera position gave me the desired perspective relationship between model and backdrop, although in this scene perspective was relatively easy. It was critical to keep the projector lens below the horizon in the scene. Otherwise, the projector light would have created a hot spot in the photo.

**JOHN OLSON 69**

(Left) With dramatic photos in mind, I chose a rock mold with a sharp, detailed texture for this waterfall area. For high contrast (to increase drama), I kept the light at a high angle to prevent opening up shadows on the rocks (look at the scenery in the lower left corner). I bracketed my shots in ½-stop increments to catch the proper light saturation while maintaining the desired sharp contrast.

(Right) A typically chaotic scene: Here, you get an idea of how crowded it can be when you're shooting a model railroad. The area is usually small, and in the midst of an exposure you're working against the clock. This was a video shoot for the Brockway Broadcasting Corporation's television documentary "The World of Photography" in 1985. I selected my Mule Shoes Meadows layout for this session. My friend Ron Dickson and I worked together on the color shot (above), using the setup that you see here.

(Above) Mishap on the Mescal Line, from MODEL RAILROADER Magazine's 50th anniversary issue, January 1984.

To achieve this special work scene on my layout, and to make use of Paul Scoles' steam shovel, I had to tear out some rock work and cover the track with loose granite. I installed the work lights and "damaged" the semaphore. The lights were necessary for the sunrise effect I desired. To emphasize the point of interest — the working steam shovel — the locomotive and backdrop were intentionally de-emphasized in both focus and lighting. I under-illuminated the locomotive and over-illuminated the backdrop. As a result, the viewer's interest flows from bottom right to upper left. This (and the train's orientation) leads the eye to the intended point of interest. I placed a backdrop light high, carefully baffling it to prevent light from spilling into the scene. A moderately wide aperture setting of f 11 causes the focus to fall off rapidly, further emphasizing the center of interest.

With complex lighting such as this, exposure times are difficult to calculate. I bracketed shots five stops over and under the meter reading.

(Left) Using a wide-angle lens can be dangerous: Distortion and a compressed foreground look artificial. I had to keep the lens plumb and horizontal while adjusting the tripod height to frame the scene. I shot from three heights, bracketing the shots at each height with four exposures.

Warm-colored railroad equipment complements the red rock scenery on this section of the Mescal Lines. I took extra care with the main light, trying it in several positions to best illuminate the variety of dried-flower foliage without having the wispy, gossamer shadow patterns confuse the image.

**JOHN OLSON 75**

(Above) The mood of this scene hints at the atmosphere created in the movie *On the Waterfront.* I intentionally used the stock-car floor as the horizon so you would feel as if you were at the end of land (or the world). Other photos of the J&S dispel the common notion that this model was incomplete (lacking distant objects). All figures are in solitary attitudes to avoid any feeling of community. The inanimate objects — power poles, auto, and crossback — also lend to the feel of loneliness. I tilted the top of the back-drop toward the camera to help the "whoosh" of the clouds draw you right through the scene and out to sea.

(Left) I call this one "Frary's Challenge." I always thought this shot was busy, but Dave Frary summed it up when he said, "I counted the people in the scene several times, and I never did come up with the same number!"

I enjoyed composing this scene, arranging all the elements of the scene — cars, locos, people — to show everything, yet not overwhelm the viewer with billions and billions of details. The intense lighting is of prime importance here: Direct overhead lights were necessary because long shadows would confuse the view by making it even more complex.

(Above) Most of the Jerome & Southwestern is in the desert. I wanted this mountain shot on the J&S to look different from my other photos of the same layout. For the appearance of a higher altitude with thin air, I used Ekta-chrome (it has a bluish hue) and kept brilliant light away from the background. The soft shadows replicate the light of high mountain passes.

I regret not installing a headlight on the loco. Without the headlight, what should be a point of interest in the picture is instead a dead spot.

**JOHN OLSON 77**

**78 JOHN OLSON**

The end of a day in Mule Shoes Meadow — and for three tired photographers. Back in 1976, Paul Scoles, Craig Bennett, and I worked all day and produced only two rolls of exposed film. Today any one of us would expose two rolls in the first 10 minutes!

(Left, top) A mood shot of a NorthWest Short Lines 4-4-0. At first glance the photo appears complex. In fact, I placed a single 250-watt light near the camera and aimed it to accent a highly reflective backdrop. I put a yellow gel directly over the lens, positioned the gel about halfway across the lens, and set the exposure for the backdrop lighting. The gel dropped the exposure value of the loco and scenery approximately two stops, creating a silhouette effect. Due to the proximity of the gel to the lens, the dividing line became a soft blur.

(Left) Behind the scenes of a popular photo, one that appeared for years in Model Rectifier's power-pack ads. It was a difficult photo to light believably (to make it look like the Arizona desert) because of the large area involved. I had to use 1,500 watts of light, placed carefully to avoid double and triple shadows, and hold a baffle over the camera while shooting (to avoid glare in the lens). Also, it was difficult to balance the light in the scene because of a low ceiling over the layout. I left the areas under the eaves of the buildings dark to convey the high-contrast look of desert daylight.

As I said before, I rate photography second to my enjoyment of model railroading. Modeling is the key here: The rock work and the rusty vehicles, contrasted with the beautiful mountain backdrop, tell a story. Bright, shiny models would ruin the effect. Besides, it's fun to beat up and weather model railroad equipment!

My friend Ed Johnson painted the crescent moon backdrop and mountain cutout profiles. The yard lights and the light on the loco are grain-of-rice bulbs; the lights in the building are grain-of-wheat bulbs. The model lights and a diffused portion of the main light share equally in illuminating the model.

Because of the blackness of the painted backdrop, direct light was needed (on the backdrop) to balance the scene. Aside from the small bulbs used in the model, there is only one light source. I used a ½-frosted gel baffle on the light so that filtered light fell on the model while direct light fell on the backdrop. Photo courtesy of *Narrow Gauge and Short Line Gazette*.

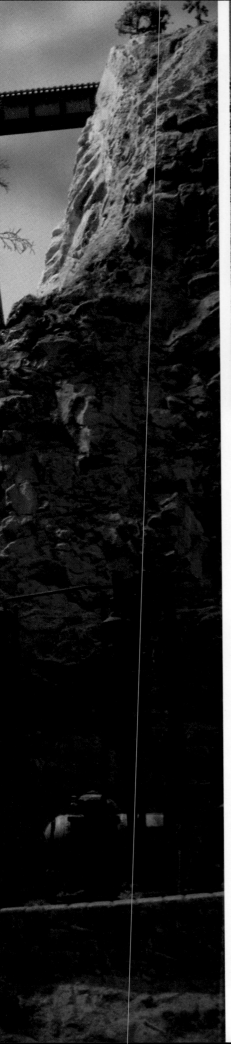

(Left) Paul Scoles writes: "John took this photo in 1975 of one of his early diorama efforts, 'Stop Gap Falls.' When I first saw this shot I detected the strong influence of legendary model railroader John Allen. The scenery is clearly Allen-influenced, as is the composition of the shot — especially the lighting.

"As Olson was learning to be a model photographer he leaned heavily on John Allen's NMRA tape/slide clinic for techniques, and those techniques are clearly evident in this shot. It was, by the way, Olson's photos of Stop Gap Falls that caught the attention of Malcolm Furlow. Malcolm was a road musician when he ran across this photo on the cover of a magazine. He was so impressed with Olson's work that he immediately began trying to model similar scenes!" Photo courtesy of *Railroad Model Craftsman*. (Above) An example of John Allen's photography: This is a scene showing part of his legendary Gorre & Daphetid layout.

This photo was taken in Willmar, Minnesota, by my wife, Katie. My grandfather was a freight agent here for some 50 years, and my father was a telegrapher/dispatcher for 17 years, both with Great Northern Ry. I was born here and spent the first four years of my life in Willmar until we moved to California in 1953.

Since 1974 I have been field art director and production designer for Walt Disney Imagineering. WDI is responsible for the creation and development of Disney theme parks — Disneyland, Walt Disney World/EPCOT, Tokyo Disneyland, and Euro Disneyland.

I've been fortunate that my career with Disney has paralleled my interest in model railroading. They feed each other. I work at Disney with some well-known train fans. They've given me quite a bit of information and interest in the hobby. Likewise, my hobby helped me get my job with Disney, since I was into a world of miniatures and fantasy.

I have been a life member of National Model Railroad Association since 1975. In 1983, Kalmbach published my book *Building An HO Model Railroad With Personality: The Jerome & Southwestern*. My work has also appeared in MODEL RAILROADER, *Railroad Model Craftsman*, NMRA Bulletin, Narrow Gauge and Short Line Gazette, and *Presse Eisenbahn*.

I want to dedicate my part of this book to Katie, who kept the coffee on while I completed this project, and to Heidi Lyn Olson, third-generation photographer.

**JOHN OLSON 83**

# The viewfinder of imagination

## PAUL SCOLES

A model railroad is art in three-dimensional form, the creation of a large picture of life and scenery as I imagine it should or could be, or perhaps as it used to be. I can create a world to my liking. Best of all, the main subjects of my artistic world, the trains, actually come to life and move.

My favorite era to portray is the 1890s, perhaps because there were no automobiles, railroads were more interesting, or maybe just because it seemed to be a happier time (those years are, after all, called the "Gay Nineties"). I have absolutely no interest in modern railroads, computers, diesels, or anything else that reminds me of the world I have to face each morning.

My modeling interests today are the same as they were 15 years ago, except that I've switched from HOn3 to Sn3. My tastes run the gamut from smooth, slow locomotive performance (micromotors, for example) to realistic scenery and scratchbuilding. My goal is to create a highly realistic miniature scene.

There are many avenues of creativity in model railroad photography, and many ways of achieving great results. We really have two forms of creativity at work here: imagining what we want to see, and being creative in our approach to getting it on film.

Of course, technique is important: You'll want to make special notes of what clever and creative things I did to reach my goal with the photograph, and also take notes on where and why I failed to get a convincing result.

However, technique is only a tool for the most important task of any photographer: transferring imagination (the vision of the mind's eye) to the reality of the camera's viewfinder. You want to be creative and daring enough to try new things, to take chances, to think. Those who are able to realize their concepts in a photograph will almost always achieve great results.

---

The techniques used in shooting this sparkling, high desert night scene on an On3 layout by Jim Rubado of Enumclaw, Washington, were dictated by necessity. A view block was needed because the town scene was surrounded by unfinished yard areas, posts, and a cluttered wall.

To add interest, I made a starry sky from a large piece of dark purple poster board with small holes in it, lighted from behind with a 300-watt bulb. I positioned the camera so it would see only the desired buildings and the sky.

A 500-watt main light, covered with a blue gel, was bounced off the ceiling to illuminate the overall scene. I painted light onto the loco front and other dark areas with a flashlight, keeping it moving constantly so the effect would be smooth and subtle.

I followed a 40-minute exposure (with all lights on) with an additional 10-minute exposure with only the loco and building lights, to allow these lights to burn in better.

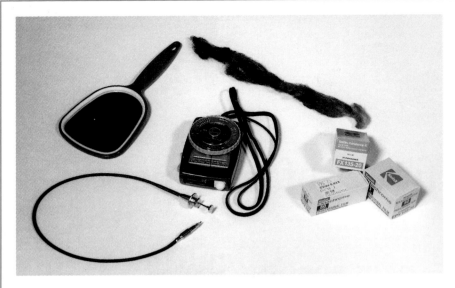

## EQUIPMENT

I use two cameras for nearly all of my model railroad photography: a 35 mm single-lens reflex (SLR), and a medium-format 2¼″ x 2¼″ twin-lens reflex.

My 35 mm camera is a basic, inexpensive Chinon model CE-4S with a stock 50 mm lens. It was given to me as a gift years ago by a lady friend who knew nothing about cameras. It's probably better that way — if I purchased my own 35 mm camera, I likely would have spent five times the money and got about the same results. Fact is, some of my best photographs have been taken with this inexpensive camera and lens.

For more demanding applications I use a Mamiya C220 (2¼″ x 2¼″ format) with an 80 mm lens (top, right). This high-quality camera has twin lenses, with the viewing lens directly above the camera lens. With this arrangement you must focus and compose close-ups through the viewing lens, then raise the camera by the exact distance between the center of the two lenses (exactly 2″ with the Mamiya C220) before taking the photograph (see diagram below, left). This parallax adjustment is one of the reasons few modelers choose twin-lens cameras for model railroad photography.

The photo above shows my small assortment of accessories. The Luna-Pro light meter is my mainstay, as I don't rely on any through-the-lens metering. Of course, I always have some painted cotton handy for replicating smoke (vital to steam subjects). A cable shutter release activates the shutter without jarring the camera and blurring the picture. Also essential to any long exposure is my Kenlock S-5 tripod.

For lighting I usually have three Smith-Victor 500-watt photofloods with reflectors, a simple hand-held mirror, and a white card to bounce light into a scene.

My film: Kodak Ektachrome 50 Tungsten for indoors, Kodak Ektachrome 64 for outdoors, and Kodak Plus-X ASA 125 or Panatomic-X ASA 32 for black-and-white.

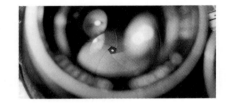

PINHOLE DIAPHRAGM

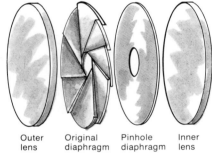

Outer lens   Original diaphragm   Pinhole diaphragm   Inner lens

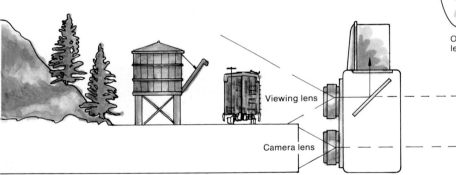

Viewing lens

Camera lens

2″

PARALLAX ADJUSTMENT

## THE PINHOLE CAMERA

Back in 1974, dissatisfied with 35 mm camera gear, I began experimenting with small-aperture photo techniques. These experiments led to fitting my Mamiya twin-lens camera with a pinhole aperture. When I look at a scene, I mentally compose it to appear with the same sense of depth and realism as is found in real life — I want my photos to convey that realism. The extended depth of field that my pinhole-adapted Mamiya delivers allows me to capture scenes as I always imagined them, but couldn't obtain with 35 mm equipment.

Studying photos of real trains reveals that depth of field is the biggest flaw in model railroad photos. In photos of real subjects, the depth of field is typically sharp from foreground to background. Although the 80 mm lens supplied with the Mamiya camera would stop down to $f$ 32, I still wasn't able to get what I considered to be realistic depth of field.

Why? Because of the physical relationship between the size and distance of real trains versus the focal length and $f$-stop (aperture) of most cameras. Cameras are usually made to photograph relatively large objects; when we try to photograph miniature scenes, the average camera can't deliver the sharp depth of field found in "real" photos.

My solution? A camera with a much smaller aperture. Others have tried pinhole cameras before, often with poor results. A notable exception was Ben King (see MODEL RAILROADER Magazine, January 1964). Rather than adding a pinhole to a 35 mm single-lens reflex camera, Ben's solution was a custom-made camera. But the complexity and expense of a camera like Ben's, and the poor results of adding a pinhole to a standard 35 mm camera, can be discouraging.

This brings me to the advantage of my Mamiya twin-lens camera. Adding a pinhole aperture to the camera lens has no effect on the viewing lens, and the resulting increase in depth of field more than offsets the hassle of having to raise the camera 2″ before snapping the photograph.

My pinhole is made from a sheet of .005″ brass, cut into a disk about the size of a quarter and measured to fit against the inside of the existing aperture diaphragm inside the lens. I marked the exact center of the disk, drilled an .024″-diameter hole, and examined the hole under a magnifying glass to ensure there were no burrs or ragged edges. Then I airbrushed the disk with a thin coat of flat black paint.

I locked the original diaphragm at $f$ 32, mounted the pinhole diaphragm flush with the inside surface of the original, and carefully centered it.

Calculating what diameter to use for a pinhole (and what $f$-stop it yields) is easy. The formula is:

$$f = \text{focal length}/\text{diameter of hole}$$

In my case this works out to:

$$f = 3.149″ \ (80 \ \text{mm})/.024″$$

The answer is 131.2 (rounded off to the nearest even $f$-stop, $f$ 128), four stops down from the $f$ 32 of the stock lens.

It takes some getting used to, but using a camera with an aperture of $f$ 128 is not difficult. Of course, longer exposures are necessary.

It's likely you will encounter an interesting phenomenon known as the reciprocity factor. Briefly: In exposures longer than a few seconds, film (especially color film) will be affected by reciprocity. The longer the film is exposed, the slower the effective film speed (ASA) becomes. I have learned to compensate by increasing my exposures by one or more $f$-stops.

Here's another key point to consider when using a twin-lens camera with a pinhole. Most twin-lens cameras focus by means of a bellows arrangement between the lens and the camera. The bellows should be used for arranging and composing the scene, but you should fully collapse it before taking the photograph.

The reason is that as the bellows is extended the focal length of the lens is increased, thereby increasing the $f$-stop of the aperture. When the bellows on my

(Above) How I'd like to haul all layouts outdoors to photograph them! Here, I did just that. This was a display layout from The Little Depot, a hobby shop in Anaheim, California. I took the photo in the shop's parking lot with a Mamiya C220 camera and an 80 mm lens at $f$ 128 for 2 seconds, with Ektachrome 64 daylight film. The layout was positioned to incorporate real trees and a real building in the frame. February midafternoon sunlight was just right. Photo courtesy of *Narrow Gauge and Short Line Gazette.*

This photo of Lonnie Shay's HOn3 Forney was taken in 1977. It's a vignette of a hot July day in a backwoods engine terminal. I shot this small diorama outdoors with a blue Masonite backdrop. During the exposure I used a mirror and a white card to direct light into deep shadows on the front of the locomotive and under the trees. Photo courtesy of *Narrow Gauge and Short Line Gazette.*

camera is fully extended, the focal length is increased to the point that my aperture is greater than *f* 512! Understandably, exposure times would be drastically altered. In fact, with my bellows fully extended the inner rings of my lens appear in the photographs: The camera is photographing its insides.

So, except for special applications, collapse the bellows before shooting. The pinhole aperture will pull the foreground into sharp focus on its own.

## THE PELICAN BAY
## RAILWAY & NAVIGATION COMPANY

The PBR&N, a narrow-gauge line running through the redwoods along the coast of Northern California, is set in the 1890s.

I began building this large HOn3 layout in the early 1970s when I lived in Southern California. It became a gathering place for friends John Olson, Lonnie Shay, T. R. Smith, and many others. Scenery, micromotors — and photography — became group efforts as we shared ideas and techniques.

Sadly, this layout was dismantled when I relocated to Seattle. But the friendships remain solid, and the flow of creativity is as strong as ever.

I've recently begun to reconstruct the Pelican Bay Railway & Navigation Company, this time in Sn3. The switch to the larger scale has rekindled my building interests and allowed me to pursue better locomotive performance, sound systems, carrier control, and other areas not feasible in HOn3.

(Above, left) Here are two experiments with backdrops, night-scene lighting, and exposures. Both scenes feature the same sky —black poster board with holes drilled in it and backlighted for the stars, and a sheet of clear Plexiglas with airbrushed clouds (see diagram, right). I suspended the backdrops from the ceiling about 18″ to 24″ behind the locomotive. The idea is to have stars shining through the clouds, giving the backdrop a three-dimensional quality. The biggest problem was keeping the main light from creating a glare on the Plexiglas.

With both the 35 mm (top left) and the 2¼″ format (above), I "burned in" the lights and stars for a few seconds before turning the main on for the rest of the exposure. The 2¼″ transparency was shot with the Mamiya C220 at *f* 128 on Ektachrome 50 film. The other photo was shot using John Olson's Nikkormat EL (a 35 mm SLR) with a 55 mm Micro Nikkor lens at *f* 32 on Ektachrome 50.

The 35 mm slide was reprocessed at a photo lab, using a blue gel filter to further enhance the photograph. The filter had an interesting effect on the clouds.

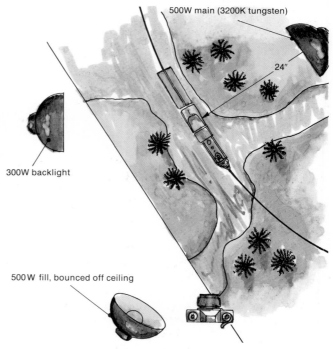

500W main (3200K tungsten)

24"

300W backlight

500 W fill, bounced off ceiling

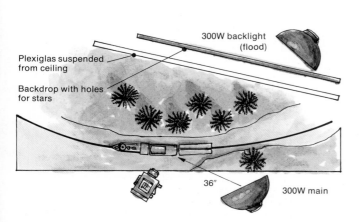

300W backlight (flood)

Plexiglas suspended from ceiling

Backdrop with holes for stars

36"

300W main

Depth and realism were my goals in this shot of the PBR&N. I placed the main light at an extreme angle to affect the whole scene, rather than just the train. To balance the scene, I bounced a 500-watt fill off the ceiling and used an additional 300-watt fill on the train. The camera is my Chinon CE-4s 35 mm SLR with a 50 mm lens; I shot at *f* 16 for ⅛ of a second with Ektachrome 50 film. Photo courtesy of *Narrow Gauge and Short Line Gazette*.

**PAUL SCOLES 89**

The same stretch of the PBR&N as seen on page 89, but with a slight change in angle, and a *big* change in lighting (diagram below). Long shadows and glowing lights alter the mood. The low light level allowed a longer exposure, so I could manipulate the cotton smoke during the exposure to make it appear to billow. Shot with the Chinon CE-4s 35 mm with 50 mm lens at *f* 16 using Ektachrome 50 film. Photo courtesy of *Narrow Gauge and Short Line Gazette*.

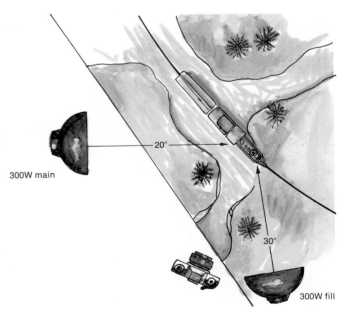

(Left) A late afternoon meet at Bennett's Creek. The lengthening shadows (created by moderate backlighting) and the glowing headlight of the locomotive draw you into this scene on the PBR&N line. For the wispy black smoke, I held black cotton over the locomotive stack and moved the cotton constantly for three minutes of the four-minute exposure.

The light meter indicated a two-minute exposure. Due to the reciprocity factor, however, one stop over (or four minutes) produced the best results.

I used the Mamiya C220 camera with an 80 mm lens at *f* 128, and Ektachrome 50 film.

I set this photograph up to demonstrate the remarkable capabilities of the pinhole aperture. I don't think a satisfactory shot of this scene can be attained with a 35 mm camera, no matter what lens is used. Sighting over the top of a train as if you were riding in the caboose cupola will quickly reveal a "normal" camera's depth-of-field shortcomings. The photograph was taken with the Mamiya C220 and 80 mm lens at f 128 for 30 seconds using Ektachrome 50 film.

(Above, below) These setup photos show the pinhole camera at work. Look at how close I am to the train — try a shot like that with a regular camera! The pinhole yields such great depth of field that both ends of the train are in focus. Note the technique for replicating smoke.

This shot of John Olson's Mule Shoes Meadows layout is one of my first published photos taken with the pinhole camera. John and I collaborated on this photograph — he set up the lighting while I handled the camera. It remains one of my favorites.

Because the only illumination in the scene was a single 250-watt tungsten bulb, a 9-minute exposure was required. I shot this photo with the Mamiya C220 and 80 mm lens at *f*128 using Ektachrome 160 tungsten film.

(Above, left) Here, the lighting portrayed a night scene while still illuminating the models. The locomotive lights were burned in for five seconds before the floods were turned on; a Vivitar cross-screen filter enhanced the loco lights. I intentionally left the background dark.

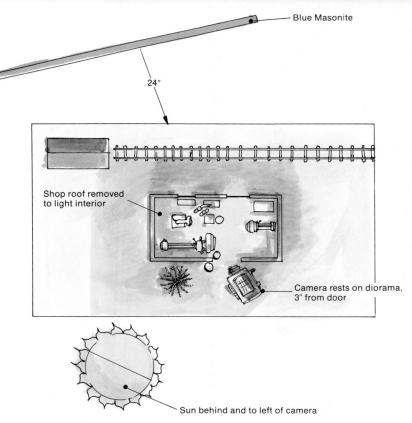

Blue Masonite

24″

Shop roof removed to light interior

Camera rests on diorama, 3″ from door

Sun behind and to left of camera

(Top right, diagram) Shot in natural sunlight, this machine shop was part of a diorama I built several years ago. The only way to get a realistic shot was to set the pinhole camera directly on the diorama and aim the lens through the door. Because scenery and structures were in the way, it was impossible to focus. I relied on the pinhole aperture to provide acceptable sharpness. The roof of the machine shop was removed to allow sunlight to illuminate the interior.

(Above, below) Here's a simple setup using two lights. The main light was above and slightly behind the locomotive to give it a crisp outline and help it stand out from the background. I used a front fill to balance the illumination, and a small mirror to reflect light on the drivers and underside of the loco. A sheet of light blue poster board, curved up at the back, formed a seamless backdrop.

(Left) This logging camp diorama by Tom Beaton of Surrey, British Columbia, was the perfect situation for the pinhole camera. A long, narrow diorama and a "down the tracks" photo angle require maximum depth of field for a realistic result; a perfect job for the pinhole camera.

Photographed with the Mamiya C220 and 80 mm lens at *f* 128 for 30 seconds using Ektachrome 50 film.

(Below) Muir Model Company used my Silver City Mine diorama for advertising back in the early 1970s. A single light source simulated the harsh, direct sunlight of the desert; I bounced light with a white fill card to soften the contrast. The hardest part was achieving the correct perspective with the HO West backdrop and the diorama.

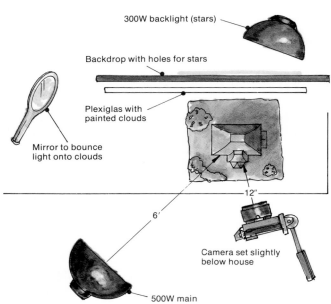

300W backlight (stars)

Backdrop with holes for stars

Plexiglas with painted clouds

Mirror to bounce light onto clouds

12″

6′

Camera set slightly below house

500W main

This is an attempt at a stormy, ethereal (perhaps even ghostly) effect, with my vintage Alexander HO Haunted House as the main prop. It's a scary shot with the photographer playing the part of mad scientist.

The sky is my trusty black poster board with holes drilled and backlighted, and clouds airbrushed on Plexiglas. As you can see in the photo of the setup, a few odd items were pressed into service for props.

During the four-minute exposure I used a small mirror to reflect light onto the clouds to highlight them. Flashing the main light once for approximately ½ second illuminated the house without washing out the backdrop.

Two 12-volt bulbs in the house provide an eerie glow. I fitted the lens with a cross-screen filter for the "crossed" points of light — an effect that almost got out of hand!

I went through a lot of film on this setup, trying a number of exposure times (with and without the cross-screen filter) and using various on-off times for the main light. Film is relatively cheap: Don't be afraid to take many different exposures, slightly altering the angle, lighting, and so forth. This is often how a good photo is realized.

Sometimes you just throw out the rules and try a shot anyway. It was impossible to aim or focus the camera, or to properly light this scene. Tom Beaton's On3 logging railroad has a beautifully detailed sawmill — but it's nearly five feet from the aisle, against a wall, and under a low ceiling! I had to simply place the Mamiya camera directly on the scenery, aim it at the sawmill, and hope the f128 pinhole would deliver acceptable focus. Lighting was another matter. Although I got adequate overall lighting with floods bounced off the ceiling (and with the layout's lights), the interior of the sawmill was still shadowy. To overcome this, I painted light into the sawmill with a flashlight during the eight-minute exposure. It was impossible to meter light for the shot accurately; I made several exposures, varying the length of the exposure and the use of the flashlight. As luck would have it, one of them worked.

(Above) To get a good shot of Tom Beaton's engine terminal and still retain the proper perspective for his beautifully painted backdrop, I again elected to place the camera directly on the layout. Shooting on a tripod from the aisle would have distorted the backdrop and spoiled the scene. I used the main layout lighting system for the overall light, with an additional 600-watt fill (bounced off the white ceiling) and a 1000-watt backlight to highlight the models and get the colors in the scene to pop.

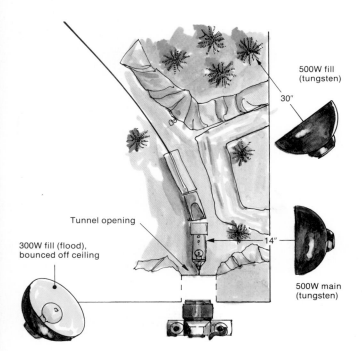

500W fill
(tungsten)

30"

Tunnel opening

300W fill (flood),
bounced off ceiling

14"

500W main
(tungsten)

(Opposite page, diagram) Shooting out of a tunnel portal can yield a dramatic and unusual view of a model railroad — and it's practically impossible unless the layout has been built with such a photo in mind. For this shot, I used John Olson's 35 mm Nikkormat EL with a 55 mm Micro Nikkor lens at f32. The hardest parts were getting enough light on the locomotive (the hill was in the way) without washing out the foreground, and lighting the distant hills adequately for equal overall illumination. Trial and error finally produced a satisfactory arrangement.

A rotary snowplow about to head for the high passes. I wanted the flat, even lighting of an overcast day, yet enough contrast for interest. I bounced both the main and fill lights off a white ceiling for an indirect light, and placed a blue gel over the fill light to cool the scene and offset the intense white created by the baking-soda snow.

I shot the scene with the Chinon 35 mm camera and 50 mm lens at *f* 16, allowing the depth of field to fall off just enough to emphasize the point of interest (the rotary).

Although simple to set up and execute, this shot did require some experimentation to get the lights just right. To help balance the light in the scene, I used a small hand-held mirror to paint light onto the rotary front and blade.

This action shot of a rotary snowplow is an idea I contemplated for a long time. The challenge of writing this book proved to be ample motivation to actually buy an Athearn HO rotary blade and housing.

Using a small can motor and rubber bands, I powered the blade so it turned at high speed, with electrical pickup through the wheels. The snow is baking soda.

Lo and behold! The rotary actually plowed the snow. The baking soda interfered with the electric pickup, so I ran a pair of small wires from the motor, under the rotary, and out of the picture.

My friend Geoff Stippes pushed the plow into the snow drift while manipulating cotton smoke, and I snapped the shutter at just the right moment. With baking soda and a tiny motor I re-created the raw power and fury of a real rotary snowplow!

I shot the photo with the Chinon CE-4s 35 mm camera and a stock 50 mm lens, using Ektachrome 160 tungsten film pushed to ASA 320. (That is, I treated the film as if it was ASA 320, and had the lab process it at 320 — twice the development time — so the exposure would be correct.) By pushing the 160 film to 320 — twice the speed — I was better able to stop the action and capture movement.

To convey depth and distance in this scene, I shot the photo over a foreground hill and down at the train. By showing the foreground and including as much scenery as possible in the composition, the small diorama seems much larger.

Overall lighting balance was critical for a natural appearance. After I placed the main and back lights, a 500-watt floodlight (bounced off the white ceiling of my den) smoothed the illumination for the desired result. Photo courtesy of *S Gaugian*.

I've been a model railroader since 1954, when I was a boy living in Kobe, Japan. My interest in model railroading is an outgrowth of my exposure at an early age to art and creativity. My mother was a famous artist, and her ability to transform bare canvas into a beautifully realistic scene stimulated my imagination. In fact, my model railroading interests and style are direct derivations of her artistic influence.

My narrow-gauge modeling dates back to 1963, when I began modeling HOn3. In the 1970s, after a long period of inactivity — due mainly to college, girls, baseball, and the Vietnam War — I pursued model railroading in earnest.

Over the last 15 years my articles have been published in *Narrow Gauge and Short Line Gazette*, MODEL RAILROADER, *Railroad Model Craftsman*, *S Gaugian*, and *Sn3 Modeler*.

I am single, avoid the question of age, a college graduate, and an avid reader. I am able to find sufficient modeling time owing to the fact that I don't own a TV. I earn my living as the owner and chief engineer of a 24-track recording studio in Seattle.